Mini Cigarillos

Martino Pedrozzi

Mini Cigarillos
Working with Oscar Niemeyer for Two Months

Lars Müller Publishers

4

I had finished my studies and had to find something to do. I bought a book entitled *Niemeyer, Architetto e poeta*[1] in an architectural bookshop. A photograph on page 406 showed the interior of Oscar Niemeyer's office, with Copacabana beach in the background, and I'd think that was where I wanted to be. I searched for the telephone number, called it and asked to speak to him. They put me through, and we had a short and friendly conversation, but the answer was no: there was a shortage of work in Brazil following a sudden economic downturn, which I had read about in our newspapers. I cursed the downturn and made peace with myself.

[illegible]

Rio, 10.06.1999

Para: Mr. Martino Pedrozzi
Fax: 00.41.91. 942-1325
De: Oscar Niemeyer
Fax: 00.55.21.267-6388

Nos. de páginas (01) incluindo esta.

J'ai reçu ton fax et je suis d'accord. Tu peux choisir les deux mois de collaboration, comme tu veux. Je te prie de me renseigner la date de ton [illegible] une semaine avant.

Cordialement,

Oscar Niemeyer

Three years passed, and I was working as an assistant to Kenneth Frampton. I told him the Niemeyer story. He was amused and said that his first monograph, purchased at the age of twenty, had been Stamo Papadaki's *The Work of Oscar Niemeyer*.[2] Frampton was keen to help and wrote a letter. The reply arrived two months later: "I have received your fax and am in favor. You can choose which two months you'd like to work. Please give me a week's prior notice of your departure date." I was over the moon.

I walked towards the departure gate for the Rio de Janeiro flight and spotted a wooden box bearing the words *Davidoff Mini Cigarillos* in the duty-free shop. It was identical to one I had seen in a Niemeyer photograph before leaving. "You never know," I thought, and bought two of them.

Three days went by, and we had lunch in his office. After coffee, it was time for a cigar, but they had run out and Niemeyer apologized. I couldn't believe it and got mine out. Niemeyer was taken aback and more incredulous than me. He looked at them and he looked at me, surprised and happy. We smoked with gusto and, when it was time to get back to work, I gave him the box.

He said I could live in the Canoas House. It was empty and only visited by the servants and gardener. I was struck by his generosity and would have liked to accept, but getting there without a car was problematic. I thanked him but found a guesthouse near the office of my own accord.

The weeks passed, and Niemeyer suddenly remembered the issue of my accommodation, left in limbo. He gazed seriously at me and asked what arrangements I had made. I told him about the guesthouse. He wanted to know how much it was costing me, but I wouldn't tell him. He insisted, asking me to write the amount on a piece of paper in front of us. I wrote it down and he took his check book out of his jacket pocket, copied the sum, signed the check, and handed it to me.

The University of Brasília building was 700 meters long, and Niemeyer had designed it in repetitive prefabricated blocks to rationalize construction. The five hundred CIEP (Centro Integrado de Educação Pública), schools he built in the 1980s in response to a national emergency for new educational structures, were also repetitive.

By contrast, the Canoas House was a one-off, and Niemeyer told me he had designed it with great care for that specific location with its irregular dip and protruding rock. He remembered what Walter Gropius had said when he had shown it to him: "Yes it's lovely, but it can't be replicated." This still perplexed Niemeyer and he said disapprovingly: "He is so mediocre."

While on the subject of illustrious colleagues, I asked: "What about Mies?" And he replied bluntly: "Repetitive." Niemeyer is often linked to Le Corbusier, yet from Brasília on I find a comparison with Mies van der Rohe more relevant.

He drew his design curves freehand, and it was up to us co-workers to translate them into the technical language of working drawings. He believed that the sculptural potential of concrete originated from its initially liquid state, whereas orthogonal forms stemmed from the practicality of constructing linear formworks. I asked him why the four fronts of the Ministry of Justice in Brasília were all different. He candidly replied: "To diversify."

Opposite page: views of the model showing the wealth of forms presented by the stadium and the four minor arenas. Below: view of the school grounds, and the well sheltered northern side of the stadium.

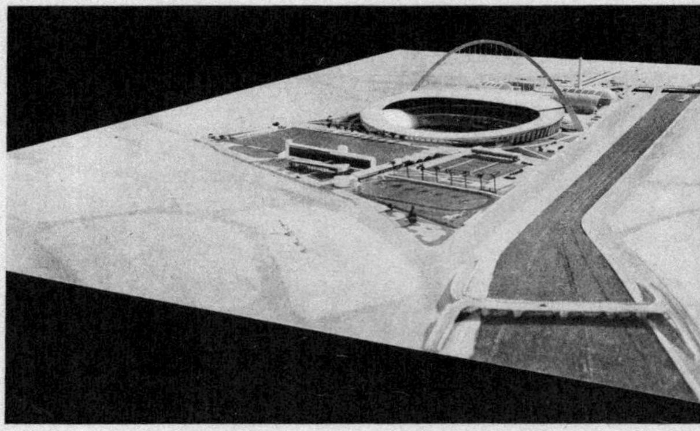

Like all good Brazilians, Niemeyer was a football fan. There was a television to watch football matches on at the back of a dark alcove in the office. One day, he spoke to me about his project for the National Stadium, which he designed in 1941 at the age of thirty-four. He criticized the shape of the stands, higher on one side: "I liked the asymmetric terraces of a Le Corbusier design and the arch of his Palace of the Soviets. But football is a collective celebration, and the playing pitch must be at the center of it." Forgivingly, he said: "Well, we were young."

On another day we were watching Germany–Brazil in the first qualifying round of the Confederations Cup, and I asked him point-blank: "Maradona or Pelé?" He hesitated and then said: "Pelé." In my mind I disagreed and thought that the "national institution" Oscar Niemeyer could not really have given any other answer.

I told Niemeyer that I wanted to visit Brasília. He replied that he had to go there in the coming days and that we could travel together by car. I was keen. It was the one thousand plus kilometer route he had covered numerous times during the works on the capital. But then the journey never happened.

Speaking about Brasília, he explained how wrong all those trees recently planted along the main axis were. I argued that a few trees would certainly not detract from that monumental space. But he was right, just compare old and recent photographs: the vegetation is reintroducing the specific savannah-like feel of the Planalto Central, the plateau on which Brasília is constructed, into an abstract esplanade that symbolizes the whole country.

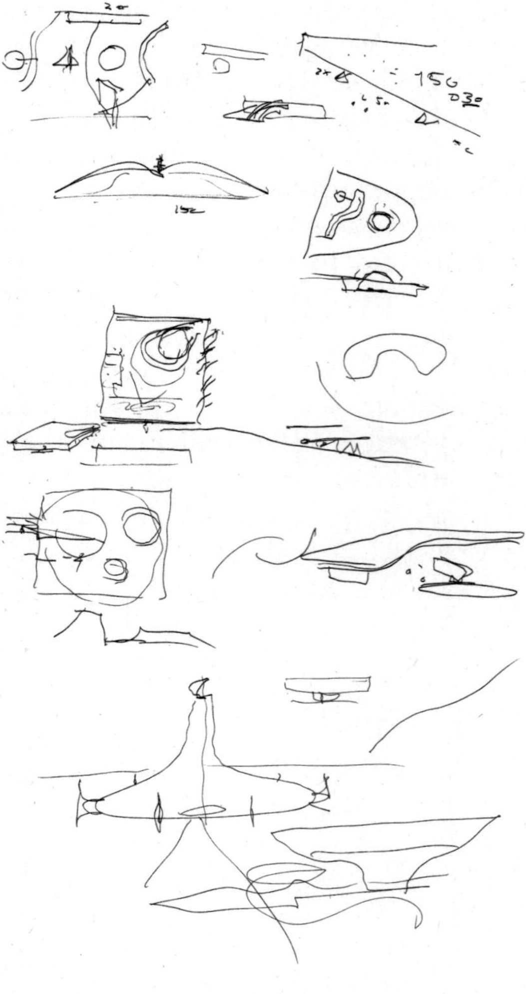

He described his projects as if he were telling a story. He explained how they originated, in what context, which people were involved, the complexities and design choices, and the end story. He illustrated his stories with drawings as he spoke. Words and images progressed hand in hand. I have carefully conserved dozens of those sketches, now without a voice.

Every year, the Japanese publisher JA+U holds an international design competition featuring a single and prestigious judge. In 1999, the judge was Niemeyer and the program he put forward was for a small theater seating two hundred people in a square measuring 100 × 40 meters. Each one of the 348 entrants presented two drawings, 696 in total. I placed them on the table one after the other during the judging process.

Niemeyer had me set the designs that interested him to one side. He discarded the others by shifting them one centimeter forward with a jerk of his fingers. Gratuitous graphic effects produced with a computer irritated him: "Silliness like this to impress people!"

If the design treated the empty space in the square as residual, he would snap: "It's garbage." He said that empty space is architecture, and a square is made of an abundance of voids. After several conventional designs, he wearily concluded: "Imagination is screwed" and he blamed schools, from primary level upwards. But, if a project delighted him, he cheered up and used uncommon words for us Europeans such as fantasy, good taste, free rein, talent and sensual.

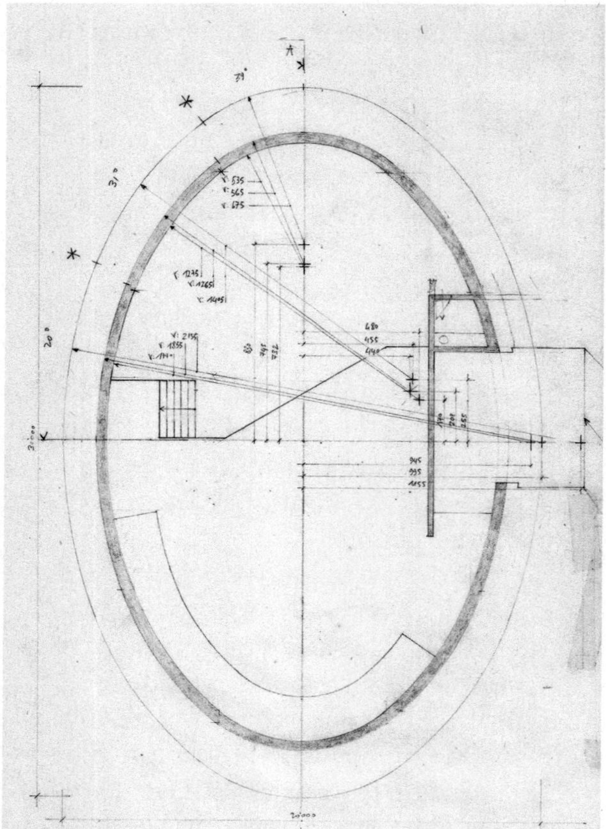

Niemeyer inaugurated the worksite for the future Popular square in Niterói: an artificial area 500 × 200 meters stolen from the sea and dotted with his buildings. These included the Roberto Silveira Memorial, on which I too was working in the office. Thinking of the string of memorials he had designed, I mischievously said: "They certainly make a lot of memorials in Brazil…" He grasped the irony and whispered: "It's all work…"

It was a Sunday and he had invited me to a family celebration at his farmstead in Bananal, on the other side of the bay. It was a grandchild's birthday. Niemeyer was the grandfather of the birthday boy's grandfather. The farmstead was a historic building just one story high, and with an annexed church. A raised porch overlooked a gently sloping clearing. There was music and people were dancing on the lawn and playing football. Niemeyer and his wife were stationed on armchairs beneath the porch. They had been married for seventy-one years.

In the middle of all the party commotion he asked me to follow him to the end of the porch from where three large, scattered boulders could be seen rising out of the lawn. "They've always seemed mysterious to me," he said pointing them out, "even when I was small."

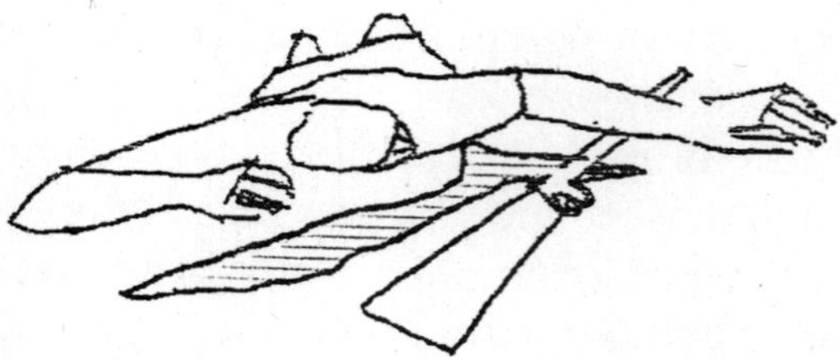

At ninety-one years of age, Niemeyer had recently completed his first work of fiction. He gave me the manuscript. It was a social critique entitled "Diante do nada" [facing nothingness]. He said he had written it "with great care," and wanted to know what I thought of it. I realized it mattered to him.

As I read, he occasionally asked me where I was to prompt a comment, or came close to me and circumspectly asked: "Is it poor?" On reaching the end, I asked: "When you have the main character say that if life deteriorates and hope leaves the hearts of men, only revolution remains, you mean..." and I mimicked a pistol with my hand. Niemeyer nodded. A few days later, while talking politics with a friend he pointed to me and good-naturedly told him: "He doesn't like scuffles."

IMPRESSO

FOLHA DE NITERÓI

www.folhanit.com.br

Preço: R$ 0,50

Ano IV • nº 220 • Semana 2 a 8 de julho de 1999 • Diretor Responsável: Luiz Antonio Mello

FIDEL CASTRO: "Os melhores amigos de Cuba estão em Niterói"

Oscar Niemeyer, Fidel Castro e Jorge Roberto Silveira

Milhares de pessoas ovacionaram o presidente de Cuba, Fidel Castro, que visitou Niterói na última quarta-feira. Sempre acompanhado do prefeito Jorge Roberto Silveira e cercado por um fortíssimo esquema de segurança, Fidel inaugurou mais um módulo do Médico de Família, no Ingá, e foi condecorado pelo prefeito no Museu de Arte Contemporânea. Emoções, lágrimas e gritos podiam ser ouvidos dos populares e dos moradores de alguns edifícios. Cobertura completa nesta edição.

ARTE DIGITAL: HILSON RICARDO / FOTOS: MAGNO MESQUITA

Niemeyer only spoke English when he had to. He didn't like the language of the North Americans. Fidel Castro had visited him a few days before my arrival in Rio de Janeiro. He spoke to me in French, the language of his Parisian exile during the years of the military regime. At the farmstead, his granddaughter had asked me whether I was offended when she called me "gringo." I answered no. And she said: "It's because Oscar told me not to do it again."

He didn't like flying. He couldn't stand the cramped space in airplanes: pressurized capsules like submarines with wings. By contrast, he loved ships: mobile minicities, floating platforms on which every person could live their own life. Niemeyer kept a careful watch over his independence, even in its most trivial aspects such as when he kicked you away if you gave him a hand climbing the stairs. His figure reminded me of his complete volumes, and the boulders scattered around the garden of the farmstead which had fascinated him as a child.

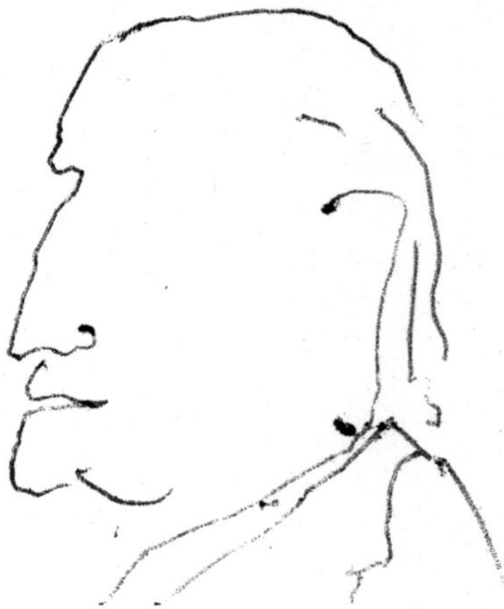

I sometimes drew him, always side-on so as not to be caught. I believed that scrutinizing the person was as crucial as studying his work.

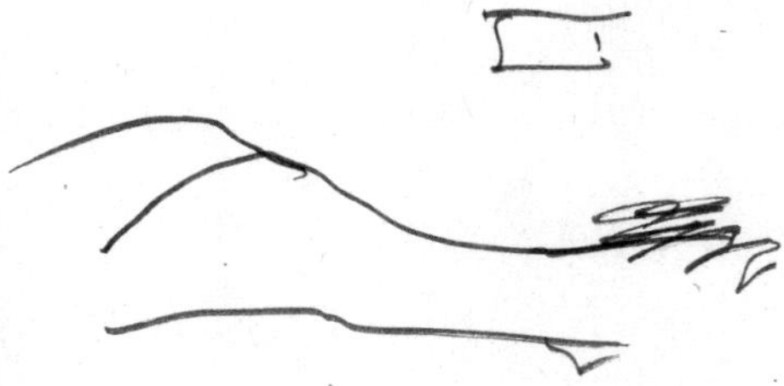

I wanted to share a part of this experience with someone. Even just so that we could remember it together when the years had passed. I invited my brothers to Rio and asked Niemeyer if I could introduce him to them. He was pleased, as I had imagined he would be.

Nicola, a doctor, gave him a recently published book of his poems. Niemeyer leafed carefully through the pages saying that he admired the Europeans' ability to cultivate several interests at the same time, commenting: "You know, only architecture is a pain." Pietro was studying civil engineering, but they did not speak just about building: "When you've spent an afternoon with a woman like this – and he sketched a reclining naked woman on a sheet of paper – you can't build a house like this," and he doodled a rectangle.

Lunch break was the best time in the office. The table was set close to a bow window facing the mouth of Guanabara Bay. At midday, the maid would spread out a white tablecloth, lay the table and bring the food. When everyone had finished, we settled in chairs with armrests, were given our own ashtrays and smoked as we chatted, sometimes only about this and that. If the conversation became mundane, Niemeyer immediately changed the subject, coming out with questions such as: "Why did the dinosaurs disappear?" "What triggered the big bang?"

On Thursdays, he organized evenings for himself and a small group of friends, inviting an expert to the office to talk about the topic that most interested him at that time. Everyone met at dinnertime, snacks were provided, and you listened to the talk. I got astrophysics.

Niemeyer told me that when he was a child, his family had owned a small house where the office block stood and that the beach was much deeper. There were unusual little shells in the sand that were not found there anymore. One sunny day he said to me: "I'd be on the beach right now if I were you." He didn't know, but I preferred the solid surface of the promenade designed by Roberto Burle Marx to the Copacabana sand, and so I did that walk in both directions nearly every evening after dinner: three kilometers each way.

Rio de Janeiro had been unusually cold for a few days; it was raining and windy. Copacabana was deserted.

Niemeyer worked in his own private space, resembling a cozy den. He was surrounded by personal keepsakes including a guitar, a portrait of Luís Carlos Prestes, a Lucien Clergue photograph, plenty of books and a small sofa for visitors. There was also a CD player and a disc with recordings of his favorite songs. The only one of all the titles handwritten on the cover I remember is Charles Aznavour's *La Bohème*.

Every now and again he stood up and walked from his sanctuary to the main office space, so bright and white it was like being outdoors. "Bad weather…" I said, and Niemeyer replied: "No, it's different weather."

We sat in the back of Niemeyer's small white Mercedes. He was so tiny that his head didn't rise above the back of the seat. Amaro was driving and had been for a lifetime. Out of affection, Niemeyer had built him a house in the favela.

We were out all afternoon in the Rio suburbs. Niemeyer visited a school of architecture in a poor neighborhood and met the students. It was raining. All you could hear was the noise of the engine and the tires turning on the wet asphalt. Niemeyer was on one side, and I was on the other. We looked out of the windows, absorbed in our thoughts. I was glad to be returning to the office. Suddenly, he turned to me and said: "I love going back to the office."

I think Oscar Niemeyer's generosity and melancholy came from the same place: an awareness that we all must go in the end. Now and again, he would stand alone before the big window with his hands in his pockets, his face so close to the glass that it disappeared. He gazed at the landscape as a whole, not one place or a particular feature. Had he not been an atheist I would have said he was observing creation. At those times, the elderly Niemeyer resembled a bystander watching the world as if it were a spectacle about to end.

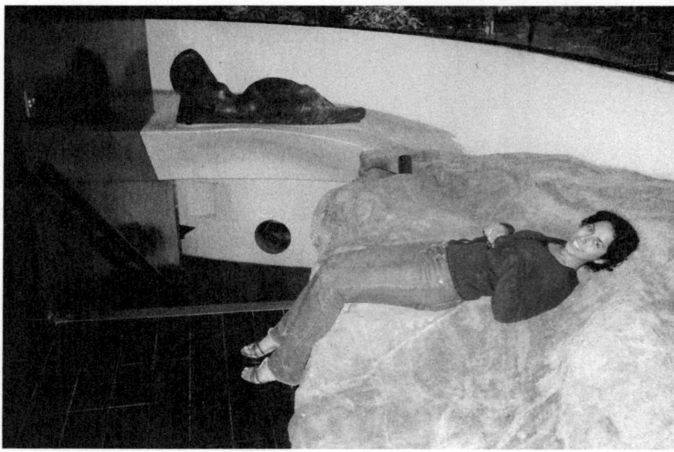

Soon, my two months in his office came to an end. Victoria joined me from Argentina, and I introduced her to him. She was beautiful. Niemeyer was pleased and asked whether we had met there, in Rio. He almost seemed to be hoping so. Amused, we had to tell him that we had met a few months earlier in Switzerland, at the school where she was studying and I was teaching.

That same day, we left by coach for Pampulha, then Brasília, São Paulo and back to Rio. In Brasília, we were greeted by a friend of Niemeyer's. Accompanied by him, we were even allowed to visit Alvorada Palace, the presidential residence. We handed our documents over at the sentry box and waited for a motorcade to pass: Fernando Henrique Cardoso, President of Brazil from 1995 to 2003, had left, and we entered.

We were struck by the presence of familiar objects such as a child's bicycle with stabilizers, and colorful plastic toys on the edge of the swimming pool in that absolute space designed by Niemeyer. As we visited the small private chapel, I thought back to when Niemeyer told me he had placed it beside the porch with his Bananal farmstead in mind.

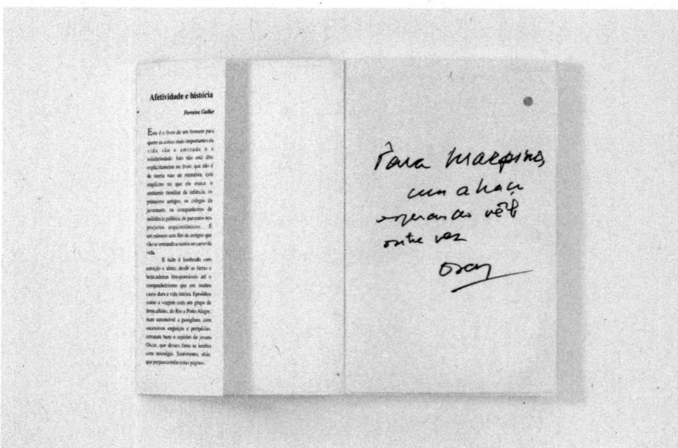
Afetividade e história
Ferreira Gullar

Back in Rio, we stopped by the office for a last goodbye and to say thank you. As we shook hands, he said: "Your presence has been much appreciated." I was touched. He wrote an inscription in his book of memoirs *The Curves of Time*:[3] "To Martino, with a hug and in the hope I'll see you again. Oscar." My sentiment too, but it never came to pass.

Notes

1 Jean Petit, *Niemeyer, Architetto e poeta* (Lugano: Fidia Edizioni d'Arte, 1995)

2 Stamo Papadaki, *The Work of Oscar Niemeyer* (New York: Reinhold, 1950)

3 Oscar Niemeyer, *The Curves of Time: The Memoirs of Oscar Niemeyer* (New York: Phaidon, 2007)

Credits

p. 4	Jean Petit, *Niemeyer, Architetto e poeta* (Lugano: Fidia Edizioni d'Arte, 1995)
p. 6	Martino Pedrozzi archive
pp. 8, 22	Photographs by Erwin Viray
pp. 10, 18, 26, 32, 38, 40, 42, 44, 50 (bottom)	Photographs by Martino Pedrozzi
p. 12	University of Brasília, photograph by Martino Pedrozzi
p. 14	The roof of Canoas House, scale 1:20, designed by the author as a coffee table, photograph by Martino Pedrozzi
p. 16	Page 47 of Stamo Papadaki, *The Work of Oscar Niemeyer* (New York: Reinhold, 1950)
p. 20	Sketches by Oscar Niemeyer, Martino Pedrozzi archive
p. 24	The author's drawing of the plan of the Roberto Silveira Memorial produced in Niemeyer's office, Martino Pedrozzi archive
p. 28	Niemeyer's drawing on the cover of the manuscript of *Diante do nada*, later published by Revan in Rio de Janeiro in late 1999, Martino Pedrozzi archive
p. 30	Front page of the weekly *Folha de Niterói* dated July 28, 1999, Martino Pedrozzi archive
p. 34	Sketch of Oscar Niemeyer by the author, Martino Pedrozzi archive
p. 36	Sketch by Oscar Niemeyer, Pietro Pedrozzi archive
p. 48	Victoria at Canoas House, photograph by Martino Pedrozzi
p. 50 (top)	Photograph by Victoria Diaz Saravia
p. 52	Photograph of Niemeyer's inscription in Oscar Niemeyer, *As curvas do tempo, Memórias* (Rio de Janeiro: Revan, 1998), Martino Pedrozzi archive

About the author

Martino Pedrozzi, born in Zurich in 1971, runs an architecture practice in Mendrisio and is a titular professor at the Accademia di architettura of the Università della Svizzera italiana.

He has published online *Primavera 2020* (www.primavera2020.ch) and the volumes *Cigarrilhas, Dois meses no escritório de Oscar Niemeyer* (São Paulo: Editora Romano Guerra, 2022); *Perpetuating architecture* (Zurich: Park Books, 2020); *Quindici edizioni di WISH, Workshop on International Social Housing* (Mendrisio: Mendrisio Academy Press, 2020); *Mini Cigarilos, Due mesi nello studio di Oscar Niemeyer* (Siracusa: Letteraventidue, 2020); *Casualità e disegno, Edilizia residenziale e spazio pubblico a Lugano* (Bellinzona: Edizioni Casagrande, 2020); *Il lido di Ascona di Livio Vacchini, Una teoria del giunto* (Bellinzona: Edizioni Casagrande, 2017). In 2020, he produced the documentary *Essere felici*.

Mini Cigarillos
Working with Oscar Niemeyer for Two Months

Author: Martino Pedrozzi
Translation: Barbara Fisher
Copyediting and proofreading: Stephanie Shellabear
Project coordination: Emilia Maier
Design: Lars Müller Publishers
Printing and binding: DZA Druckerei zu Altenburg, Germany
Paper: Holmen Trend 2.0, 80 g/m²

Lars Müller Publishers is supported by the Swiss Federal Office of Culture with a structural contribution for the years 2021–2025.

Lars Müller Publishers
Pfingstweidstrasse 6, 8005 Zurich, Switzerland
+41 44 274 37 40
info@lars-mueller-publishers.com
www.lars-mueller-publishers.com

Product safety
Producer: Lars Müller Publishers GmbH
Responsible person in accordance with EU Regulation 2023/988 (GPSR): Michael Klein, sales representative, Hub 1, DE-84149 Velden
+49 8742 964 552 2, gpsr@lars-mueller-publishers.com

ISBN 978-3-03778-808-0

Distributed in North America, Latin America and the Caribbean by ARTBOOK | D.A.P.
www.artbook.com

Printed in Germany